About the auth

Katharine Otter is an energetic, motivated and ambitious professional. Committed to the success and achievement of children across the whole school and to the development of both staff and students. Proven track record of successful leadership. A visible and vigilant leader through modelling and by example. Believes that children deserve the best education.

Katharine started an educational company called LessonSource because she felt that too often, chance, luck and coincidence can be the make or break of a great education. Katharine recognised that in today's teaching world, there is never enough time – but children's education is too precious for this to become an excuse. Her company, LessonSource provide high quality lesson bundles that, no matter what, create every chance that children will get a great lesson. Of course, the added bonus is that teachers also get back a whole load of time because all lessons and materials are provided, ready and waiting to be used.

With over 10 years of teaching experience with 4 at senior leadership level, she is very familiar with the time and energy that goes into preparing lessons. Every teacher does seem to be trying to reinvent the wheel. Now there is a better solution. LessonSource prepare high quality lesson bundles. The whole package; teacher presentation, interactive resources, worksheets, support cards, everything. It's thoroughly planned out for the whole year, so when you subscribe to a bundle you get 39 lessons of high quality content.

If you have any questions or comments, please email Katharine Otter at otter.k@lessonsource.co.uk

CONTENTS

1. DELIVERING SMSC
2. SMSC GUIDANCE
3. LONG TERM, WHOLE SCHOOL
4. LESSON OBSERVATIONS
5. TEACHING
6. PROMOTING BRITISH VALUES
7. DEMOCRACY
8. THE RULE OF LAW
9. INDIVIDUAL LIBERTY
10. MUTUAL RESPECT AND TOLERANCE OF THOSE WITH DIFFERENT FAITHS AND BELIEFS
11. TEACHING RIGHT FROM WRONG
12. BRITISH VALUES BEST PRACTICE
13. THINKING BIG
14. DIVERSITY
15. THE PREVENT STRATEGY

16. CHANNEL DUTY GUIDANCE

17. PREVENT FOR SCHOOLS

18. DELIVERING PREVENT IN SCHOOLS

19. ASSEMBLY DELIVERY

20. ASSEMBLY CONTENT

21. CLOSING WORDS

DELIVERING SMSC

SPIRITUAL, MORAL, SOCIAL AND CULTURAL DEVELOPMENT

Developing students spiritually, morally, socially and culturally (SMSC) has never been so important. A great education should cover these aspects regardless of what Ofsted or government policy dictate. However, there is a fair amount of guidance on the back of Ofsted inspections and DfE have dictated that various aspects are covered as a part of the overall student experience and curriculum.

SMSC GUIDANCE

The Ofsted inspection handbook (p34) defines and explains how SMSC development should be shown and the DfE detail how British values should be promoted as a part of SMSC we also offer advice on delivering British values here. Developing outstanding SMSC has to be a process over time; it is not about reciting list of facts or processes. SMSC is a deeper, fundamental concept, which needs to be nurtured throughout a child's education.

LONG TERM, WHOLE SCHOOL

Having a clear, long term plan for how and when spiritual, moral, social and cultural development will take place is essential. Events and experiences need to be planned, from year 7 through to year 13.

CROSS CURRICULA TRACKING

While a some aspects of SMSC development can be delivered through a range of curriculum subjects, it's important to keep an up-to-date, cross curricula tracking map (available here). With new Ofsted and DfE guidance on British values, more and more schools are now opting to deliver a timetabled, weekly lesson of SMSC, often in combination with PSHE. To ease planning and resource provision, lesson content packages are often bought in from external providers.

LESSON OBSERVATIONS

SMSC should also be tracked on lesson observations; percentages of lessons evidencing SMSC, and percentages of good or better lessons with SMSC. A lot of observations are now electronic which can make it easy to track SMSC performance. Teachers should track their own performance of SMSC for their professional development files, especially when nearing pay grade threshold, or on performance related pay. Heads of department or faculty must also maintain an overview of SMSC performance within their subject, as must the Senior leadership team in order to maintain a clear whole school overview of SMSC.

TEACHING

No matter what you teach, you are responsible for delivering SMSC, it's essential to stay tuned to the spiritual, moral, social and cultural development of your students and look out for opportunities to discuss issues that impact on your students lives. There can be pressure on teachers to produce results, which can make lesson time become overly focused on subject content, leaving wider issues unaddressed. For example DT teachers should look for opportunities to design around cultures and when making, the ethics of sustainability can readily be addressed. However, often teachers are asked to deliver SMSC or PSHE as a part of their timetabled teaching commitment. Planning for this in schools can be difficult but there are plenty of places to find great lessons and resources to suit the needs of your students. SMSC is becoming a subject in it's own right but because it is delivered by teachers across a whole school and not one small faculty, consistency in delivery and resource preparation can be difficult to co-ordinate, which is why so many schools opt to use externally provided resources.

PROMOTING BRITISH VALUES

"Schools should promote the fundamental British values of democracy, the rule of law, individual liberty, and mutual respect and tolerance of those with different faiths and beliefs"
DFE page 5

BRITISH VALUES

As a part of the The Prevent strategy, schools must promote the fundamental British values through SMSC. According to the DfE, the British values are:

- Democracy
- The rule of law
- Individual liberty
- Mutual respect and tolerance of those with different faiths and beliefs

DEMOCRACY

Through teaching students about democracy, students should develop an understanding of how citizens can influence decision-making through the democratic process. This is often delivered through the formation of student voice, ensuring that students have full involvement of the democratic process of electing representatives and the the student council supports the decision making processes in school.

THE RULE OF LAW

Schools should teach students an appreciation that living under the rule of law protects individual citizens and is essential for their wellbeing and safety. This is often achieved through behaviour models that promote student participation, ensuring that students welcome the benefits of rules in their learning environment. Students should also develop an understanding that there is a separation of power between the executive and the judiciary, and that while some public bodies such as the police and the army can be held to account through Parliament, others such as the courts maintain independence.

INDIVIDUAL LIBERTY

Through SMSC, the British value of individual liberty should promote understanding that the freedom to choose and hold other faiths and beliefs is protected in law. Students should be encouraged to explore their own cultures and beliefs and develop understanding and respect of those of others.

MUTUAL RESPECT AND TOLERANCE OF THOSE WITH DIFFERENT FAITHS AND BELIEFS

Students should have an acceptance that other people having different faiths or beliefs to oneself (or having none) should be accepted and tolerated, and should not be the cause of prejudicial or discriminatory behaviour. They should also have an understanding of the importance of identifying and combatting discrimination. This is often developed through SMSC and PSHE lessons involving education on a range of faiths and belief, with a range of role playing activities to enhance understanding of different faiths and beliefs.

TEACHING RIGHT FROM WRONG

The way of living has changed significantly and continues to evolve rapidly. Children, as well as adults, are now exposed to a wide range of media. Even with the best parental locks, children will become exposed to sensitive material at an age which we may preferred them to remain unexposed. Families no longer have the sole responsibility instilling a sense of morality in the next generation, it is also the responsibility of educators. As educators, we must ensure that children become fully rounded members of society who treat others with respect and tolerance, regardless of background as outlined in the November 2014 DfE press release. One of the greatest qualities of Britain is the cultural diversity across the country. It is essential that teachers inspire understanding of the significance of our democratic society and embrace cultural differences.

BRITISH VALUES BEST PRACTICE

The best schools form a school council or student voice, with elected representatives from a variety of ages and backgrounds, who meet regularly as a group and with key senior leadership staff to influence school decisions.

In addition, provision of specific learning activities to discuss the advantages and disadvantages of democracy should be planned. Lessons also provide opportunities for students to apply their understanding of democracy and British values by defending and questioning points of view. Lessons are popularly extended as an extracurricular activity. The DfE offer detailed guidance on how British values should be promoted as a part of SMSC development and state that the fundamental British values are **democracy**, the **rule of law,** individual **liberty**, and mutual **respect** and **tolerance** of those with different faiths and beliefs. These should be promoted through SMSC.

THINKING BIG

The world is a smaller place. The youth of today live within a United Nations government in addition to the UK government. Teachers are educating students to think bigger. Sequences of lessons are planned to explore the impact of decisions on other countries around the world without being limited to our own. Dedicated planning for the promotion of British values is imperative as is the monitoring and tracking of this as a part of SMSC. To improve the quality of resources for promoting British values as a part of SMSC, many schools opt to deliver lessons using high quality resources from external providers to ensure that their students development needs are properly met and British values are delivered.

DIVERSITY

Despite modern advances, millions of people still live in areas of danger and conflict, without sufficient food or shelter and immigration has made the headlines once again. A good curriculum creates specific opportunities for students to develop empathy and understanding around these issues. Opportunities to understand UK poverty defined as around £200 per week after living costs, contrasting international definitions of approximately £10 per week should be included. Students need to learn about how lucky they are to be a part of Great Britain and embrace the diversity and British values that makes it so great.

THE PREVENT STRATEGY

The government prevent strategy was brought into practice due to the UK level if threat from international terrorism being analysed as severe (4th highest out of the 5 levels). The most significant terrorist threats to the UK come from Al Qa'ida based in Afghanistan and Pakistan. The Home Office work to counter terrorism based on 4 areas- pursue, prevent, protect and prepare and the prevent strategy includes working with schools and other educational establishments to prevent extremism.

"There have been allegations that a minority of independent faith schools have been actively promoting views that are contrary to British values, such as intolerance of other cultures and gender inequality. There have also been reports that some independent faith schools have allowed extremist views to be expressed by staff, visitors or pupils". *Prevent strategy*

Over the last few years in England, the DfE engaged in a range of Prevent-related initiatives through a dedicated Prevent team. Following an informal consultation process with headteachers and local authority children's services they published a toolkit to help schools prevent 'violent extremism'.

CHANNEL DUTY GUIDANCE

The Channel duty guidance protects vulnerable people from being drawn into terrorism. Channel ensures that vulnerable children and adults of any faith, ethnicity or background receive support before their vulnerabilities are exploited by those that would want them to embrace terrorism, and before they become involved in criminal terrorist related activity

PREVENT FOR SCHOOLS

Schools can prevent extremism though:

- A curriculum which is adapted to recognise local needs, challenge extremist narratives and promote universal rights
- Teaching and learning strategies which explore controversial issues in a way which promotes critical analysis and pro-social values
- The use of external programmes or groups to support learning while ensuring that the input supports the college goals and values

The aim is to ensure students become responsible citizens, confident individuals and successful learners.

Partially, this is about recognising opportune moments to discuss opinions and views of students and offer appropriate guidance and challenge. However, it is more proactive to have a defined curriculum or schedule of educational events to ensure that all students are educated about extremism. At the same time it is important not to misrepresent extremism. When the scheme first came into play, there were a few governmental policy disasters along the way which stigmatised muslims. The BBC published an interesting article on this.

DELIVERING PREVENT IN SCHOOLS

In 2014 the DfE introduced guidance to promote British values as a part of SMSC. This encourages education about respect and tolerance as well as law, democracy and liberty. And yes, all of this is to be taught in addition to the standard curriculum. While afternoons or whole days off timetable can be utilised to deliver these key messages, the best practice is to dedicate regular time to educate students about a wider range of issues that our society now face. Combining this lesson with other aspects of SMSC and or PSHE creates an effective education for students. As SMSC and PSHE are often delivered by all staff, good practice to ensure high standards and consistency is to use prepared material and resources which can be supplemented with additional materials if necessary.

ASSEMBLY DELIVERY

School assemblies are a hugely important part of the school day, whether you deliver to a class, year group or whole school, it's the best opportunity to motivate and inspire students and, perhaps most importantly, your team of staff

STARTING ASSEMBLIES

Have some music at the start of the assembly to set the theme. Don't forget to listen to every word before hand, often lyrics aren't quite as you remember them! Have this playing as students enter, so you can ensure that they arrive in an orderly fashion and those that are early are engaged and excited about what's going to come next.

STUDENT INVOLVEMENT

Get the students involved- whether it's year group or whole school assemblies. Seek out a couple of outgoing students in advance and provide them with prompt cards or similar to read from during your assembly. Ideally, gather them them day before to have them practice reading the material and give them a few pointers. By using students to help lead the assembly, their peers will naturally become more engaged, plus the students that perform will grown in confidence. Remember to reward them too!

Remember that the assembly space is much bigger than a classroom so you will need to project your voice more than usual. Ask a colleague to stand at the back and give you a signal to speak up if need be.

ASSEMBLY CONTENT

Use a visual presentation to explain your message, this will help in many ways. Firstly, it will prompt you with what to say. You can even use the notes section on most slideshow presenters to add more detail. On that note, keep text on the slides minimal or everyone will be reading the screen rather than listening to what you're saying! Use the time you are in front of your students to deliver a message that you feel is truly important. This is valuable time with them. View assembly duty as a great opportunity and get excited about it. Let your enthusiasm shine through too.

When it's all over (phew!) don't forget to dismiss the students in an orderly way. It can help to have music playing again, or perhaps a relative video clip, so that students that have to wait until last are still engaged.

Preparing for assemblies- weekly or daily can be a time consuming task, especially when a high standard of content and resources is required every time. That's why more schools are opting to use prepared assemblies from external providers- to ensure that content is well thought out for the full year and covers a full range of topical content, in line with government guidance

PRAISE

Assembly delivery is the time for communicating. Fantastic assemblies use these valuable minutes to motivate and inspire not only students but also staff. Assemblies praise and reward, showing off how well individuals and groups are performing, highlighting achievements (don't forget the staff!). The whole room should be filled with a buzz. Don't fall into the trap of using it as an excuse to go over sanctions for the minority of students who are not yet fully engaged in the school behaviour system. However, it is a great opportunity to celebrate school values. If there are issues with behaviour that need addressing, look for ways to address this in a positive way. High-light great examples of behaviour and make sure that at least 80% of the time is spent focusing on positive aspects.

SMSC ASSEMBLIES

Spiritual, moral, social and cultural development is highly important to education right now. Assemblies are a way of consolidating SMSC learning that is already taking place through additional curricula activities. It's a great way to share good practice and allow students to lead their own learning and development. As well as promoting British values, assembly delivery is a fantastic opportunity to promote and link in the school values. Assembly time should also be used to promote events and activities that students are organising through the student council; a part of effective SMSC

CLOSING WORDS FROM KATHARINE OTTER

Thank you for reading the LessonSource SMSC practical teaching advice for secondary schools short book. I hope that you have enjoyed reading them and most importantly I hope that you (and your students) enjoy the benefit.

Teaching is a tough job and through LessonSource, I hope to make it more manageable by providing great teaching content and activity day resources. At the time of publishing LessonSource specialise in PSHE and SMSC but hope to widen the range of products. Please email me with any ideas or suggestions you have. I always try to incorporate feedback into LessonSource work.

If you have any questions or want some further advice about delivering SMSC, PSHE or British values, email info@lessonsource.co.uk or visit www.lessonsource.co.uk

Thank you and GOOD LUCK!

Printed in Great Britain
by Amazon